CW00956644

Contents

Page

6   Employment

7   Particular provisions

8   Resolving disagreements within the employing organisation   58

Purpose and status of the Code

1.1   Pages 3 to 58 are a Code of Practice issued by the Secretary of State for Education and Employment under section 53 (1) (a) of the Disability Discrimination Act 1995 ("the Act"). The Code comes into effect on 2 December 1996.

1.2   The employment provisions of the Act and the Disability Discrimination (Employment) Regulations 1996 protect disabled people, and people who have been disabled, from discrimination in the field of employment. Although the Code is written in terms of "disabled" people, it also applies to people who no longer have a disability but have had one in the past. The date from which the employment provisions take effect is 2 December 1996 (but see paragraph 7.12). The Code of Practice gives practical guidance to help employers and others – including trade organisations and people who hire staff from employment businesses – in eliminating discrimination and should assist in avoiding complaints to industrial tribunals.

1.3   The Code applies in England, Scotland and Wales. It does not itself impose legal obligations and is not an authoritative statement of the law. Authoritative interpretation of the Act and regulations is for the tribunals and courts. However, the Code is admissible in evidence in any proceedings under the Act before an industrial tribunal or court. If any provision in the Code appears to the tribunal or court to be relevant to a question arising in the proceedings, it must be taken into account in determining that question.

Using the Code

1.4   The Code describes – and gives general guidance on – the main employment provisions of the Act in paragraphs 4.1 to 4. 66. More specific guidance on how these provisions operate in different situations is in later paragraphs but it may be necessary to refer back to the general guidance occasionally. For example, someone thinking of recruiting new staff will need to read paragraphs 5.1 to 5.29 and also, unless already familiar with it, the general guidance on the provisions in paragraphs 4.1 to 4.66. Someone dealing with a new or existing employee should read paragraphs 6.1 to 6.23, again with reference to the general guidance as necessary. Examples of how the Act is likely to work in practice are given in boxes (see also paragraph 3.1). Annexes 1–3 are not part of the Code but include information on related subjects. There is a detailed index at the end of the Code.

1.5   References to the legal provisions relevant to the guidance in the Code are generally just on the first, or only, main mention of a provision. For example, "S5(1)" means Section 5, subsection (1) of the Act. "Sch 1 Para 1 (1)" means Schedule 1, paragraph 1 subparagraph (1) of the Act.

1.6   References in footnotes to "Employment Regulations" mean The Disability Discrimination (Employment) Regulations 1996 and to "Definition Regulations" mean The Disability Discrimination (Meaning of Disability) Regulations 1996.

1.7   In the examples, references to male and female individual disabled people are given for realism. All other references are masculine for simplicity but could, of course, apply to either sex.

2 Who is, and who is not, covered by the employment provisions

What is the main purpose of the employment provisions of the Act?

2.1   The Act protects disabled people from discrimination in the field of employment. As part of this protection employers may have to make "reasonable adjustments" if their employment arrangements or premises place disabled people at a substantial disadvantage compared with non-disabled people. These provisions replace the quota scheme, the designated employment scheme and registration as a disabled person *(S61(7))*.

2.2   The Act does not prohibit an employer from appointing the best person for the job. Nor does it prevent employers from treating disabled people more favourably than those without a disability.

Who has rights or obligations under the Act?

2.3   Disabled people have rights under the Act, as do people who have had disabilities but have fully or largely recovered. The Act defines a disabled person as someone with a physical or mental impairment which has a substantial and long-term adverse effect on his ability to carry out normal day-to-day activities *(S1 and Sch1)*. (See Annex 1)

2.4   The following people and organisations may have obligations under the Act:

- employers;

- the Crown (including Government Departments and Agencies) *(S64)*;

- employees and agents of an employer;

- landlords of premises occupied by employers;

- people who hire contract workers;

- trustees or managers of occupational pension schemes;

- people who provide group insurance schemes for an employer's employees;

- trade organisations.

2.5   This Act does not confer rights on people who do not have – and have not had – a disability, with the exception of the provisions covering victimisation (see paragraphs 4.53 and 4.54).

Who does not have obligations or rights under the Act?

2.6   The employment provisions do not apply to employers with fewer than 20 employees *(S7)*. The Act applies when an employer has 20 or more employees in total, regardless of the size of individual workplaces or branches. However, if the number of employees falls below 20 the employer will be exempted for as long as there are fewer than 20 employees. Independent franchise holders are exempt if they employ fewer than 20 people even if the franchise network has 20 or more employees. The Government must carry out a review of the threshold for the exclusion of small firms within 5 years of the employment provisions coming into force.

2.7   The employment provisions do not apply to:

- members of the Armed Forces *(S64(7))*;

- prison officers *(S64(5)(b))*;

- firefighters *(S64(5)(c) and (6))*;

- employees who work wholly or mainly outside Great Britain *(S68(2))*;

- employees who work on board ships, aircraft or hovercraft *(S68(3))*;

- members of the Ministry of Defence Police, the British Transport Police, the Royal Parks Constabulary and the United Kingdom Atomic Energy Authority Constabulary *(S68(5)(a)); and*

- other police officers who are in any event not employees as defined in *S68(1)*.

Who counts as an employee under the Act?

2.8   "Employment" means employment under a contract of service or of apprenticeship, or a contract personally to do any work *(S68)*. The last category covers persons who are self-employed and agree to perform the work personally. "Employee" means anyone whose contract is within that definition of employment, whether or not, for example, he works full-time.

Be flexible

3.1   There may be several ways to avoid discrimination in any one situation. Examples in this Code are *illustrative only*, to indicate what should or should not be done in those and other broadly similar types of situations. They cannot cover every possibility, so it is important to consider carefully how the guidance applies in any specific circumstances. **Many ways of avoiding discrimination will cost little or nothing**. The Code should not be read narrowly; for instance, its guidance on recruitment might help avoid discrimination when promoting employees.

Do not make assumptions

3.2   It will probably be helpful to talk to each disabled person about what the real effects of the disability might be or what might help. There is less chance of a dispute where the person is involved from the start. Such discussions should not, of course, be conducted in a way which would itself give the disabled person any reason to believe that he was being discriminated against.

Consider whether expert advice is needed

3.3   It is possible to avoid discrimination using personal, or in-house, knowledge and expertise, particularly if the views of the disabled person are sought. The Act does not oblige anyone to get expert advice but it could help in some circumstances to seek independent advice on the extent of a disabled person's capabilities. This might be particularly appropriate where a person is newly disabled or the effects of someone's disability become more marked. It may also help to get advice on what might be done to change premises or working arrangements, especially if discussions with the disabled person do not lead to a satisfactory solution. Annex 2 gives information about getting advice or help.

Plan ahead

3.4   Although the Act does not require an employer to make changes in anticipation of ever having a disabled applicant or employee, nevertheless when planning for change it could be cost-effective to consider the needs of a range of possible future disabled employees and applicants. There may be helpful improvements that could be built into plans. For example, a new telecommunications system might be made accessible to deaf people even if there are currently no deaf employees.

Promote equal opportunities

3.5   If an employer has an equal opportunities policy or is thinking of introducing one, it would probably help to avoid a breach of the Act if that policy covered disability issues. Employers who have, and follow, a good policy – including monitoring its effectiveness – are likely to have that counted in their favour by a tribunal if a complaint is made. But employers should remember that treating people equally will not always avoid a breach of the Act. An employer may be under a duty to make a reasonable adjustment. This could apply at any time in the recruitment process or in the course of a disabled person's employment.

Discrimination

What does the Act say about discrimination?

4.1 ***The Act makes it unlawful*** for an employer to discriminate against a disabled person in the field of employment ***(S4). The Act says*** "discrimination" occurs in two ways.

4.2 One way in which discrimination occurs is when:

- ■ for a reason which relates to a disabled person's disability, the employer treats that disabled person less favourably than the employer treats or would treat others to whom the reason does not or would not apply; *and*

- ■ the employer cannot show that this treatment is justified ***(S5(1))***.

> A woman with a disability which requires use of a wheelchair applies for a job. She can do the job but the employer thinks the wheelchair will get in the way in the office. He gives the job to a person who is no more suitable for the job but who does not use a wheelchair. The employer has therefore treated the woman *less favourably* than the other person because he did not give her the job. The treatment was *for a reason related to the disability* – the fact that she used a wheelchair. And the reason for treating her less favourably *did not apply to the other person* because that person did not use a wheelchair.
>
> If the employer could not justify his treatment of the disabled woman then he would have unlawfully discriminated against her.

> An employer decides to close down a factory and makes all the employees redundant, including a disabled person who works there. This is not discrimination as the disabled employee is not being dismissed for a reason which relates to the disability.

4.3 A disabled person may not be able to point to other people who were actually treated more favourably. However, it is still "less favourable treatment" if the employer would give better treatment to someone else to whom the reason for the treatment of the disabled person did not apply. This comparison can also be made with other disabled people, not just non-disabled people. For example, an employer might be discriminating by treating a person with a mental illness less favourably than he treats or would treat a physically disabled person.

4.4   The other way **the Act says** that discrimination occurs is when:

■ an employer fails to comply with a duty of reasonable adjustment imposed on him by section 6 in relation to the disabled person; *and*

■ he cannot show that this failure is justified **(S5(2))**.

4.5   The relationship between the duty of reasonable adjustment and the need to justify less favourable treatment is described in paragraphs 4.7–4.9. The duty itself is described from paragraph 4.12 onwards and the need to justify a failure to comply with it is described in paragraph 4.34.

What will, and what will not, be justified treatment?

4.6   **The Act says** that less favourable treatment of a disabled person will be justified only if the reason for it is both material to the circumstances of the particular case *and* substantial **(S5(3))**. This means that the reason has to relate to the individual circumstances in question and not just be trivial or minor.

> Someone who is blind is not shortlisted for a job involving computers because the employer thinks blind people cannot use them. The employer makes no effort to look at the individual circumstances. A general assumption that blind people cannot use computers would not in itself be a material reason – it is not related to the particular circumstances.

> A factory worker with a mental illness is sometimes away from work due to his disability. Because of that he is dismissed. However, the amount of time off is very little more than the employer accepts as sick leave for other employees and so is very unlikely to be a substantial reason.

> A clerical worker with a learning disability cannot sort papers quite as quickly as some of his colleagues. There is very little difference in productivity but he is dismissed. That is very unlikely to be a substantial reason.

> An employer seeking a clerical worker turns down an applicant with a severe facial disfigurement solely on the ground that other employees would be uncomfortable working alongside him. This will be unlawful because such a reaction by other employees will not in itself justify less favourable treatment of this sort – it is not substantial. The same would apply if it were thought that a customer would feel uncomfortable.

An employer moves someone with a mental illness to a different workplace solely because he mutters to himself while he works. If the employer accepts similar levels of noise from other people, the treatment of the disabled person would probably be unjustified – that level of noise is unlikely to be a substantial reason.

Someone who has psoriasis (a skin condition) is rejected for a job involving modelling cosmetics on a part of the body which in his case is severely disfigured by the condition. That would be lawful if his appearance would be incompatible with the purpose of the work. This is a substantial reason which is clearly related – material – to the individual circumstance.

4.7 **The Act says** that less favourable treatment cannot be justified where the employer is under a duty to make a reasonable adjustment but fails (without justification) to do so, *unless* the treatment would have been justified even after that adjustment *(S5(5))*.

An employee who uses a wheelchair is not promoted, solely because the work station for the higher post is inaccessible to wheelchairs – though it could readily be made so by rearrangement of the furniture. If the furniture had been re-arranged, the reason for refusing promotion would not have applied. The refusal of promotion would therefore not be justified.

An applicant for a typing job is not the best person on the face of it, but only because her typing speed is too slow due to arthritis in her hands. If a reasonable adjustment – perhaps an adapted keyboard – would overcome this, her typing speed would not in itself be a substantial reason for not employing her. Therefore the employer would be unlawfully discriminating if on account of her typing speed he did not employ her and provide the adjustment.

An employer refuses a training course for an employee with an illness which is very likely to be terminal within a year because, even with a reasonable adjustment to help in the job after the course, the benefits of the course could not be adequately realised. This is very likely to be a substantial reason. It is clearly material to the circumstances. The refusal of training would therefore very likely be justified.

> Someone who is blind applies for a job which requires a significant amount of driving. If it is not reasonable for the employer to adjust the job so that the driving duties are given to someone else, the employer's need for a driver might well be a substantial reason for not employing the blind person. It is clearly material to the particular circumstances. The non-appointment could therefore be justified.

How does an employer avoid unlawful discrimination?

4.8   An employer should not treat a disabled employee or disabled job applicant less favourably, for a reason relating to the disability, than others to whom that reason does not apply, unless that reason is material to the particular circumstances and substantial. If the reason is material and substantial, the employer may have to make a reasonable adjustment to remove it or make it less than substantial *(S5(3) and (5))*.

4.9   Less favourable treatment is therefore justified if the disabled person cannot do the job concerned, and no adjustment which would enable the person to do the job (or another vacant job) is practicable *(S5(3) and (5))*. (See paragraph 4.20 for examples of adjustments which employers may have to make.)

4.10 *The Act says* that some charities (and Government-funded supported employment) are allowed to treat some groups of disabled people more favourably than others. But they can do this only if the group being treated more favourably is one with whom the charitable purposes of the charity are connected and the more favourable treatment is in pursuance of those purposes (or, in the case of supported employment, those treated more favourably are severely disabled people whom the programme aims to help) *(S10)*.

What does the Act say about helping others to discriminate?

4.11 *The Act says* that a person who knowingly helps another to do something made unlawful by the Act will also be treated as having done the same kind of unlawful act *(S 57(1))*.

> A recruitment consultant engaged by an engineering company refuses to consider a disabled applicant for a vacancy, because the employer has told the consultant that he does not want the post filled by someone who is "handicapped". Under the Act the consultant could be liable for aiding the company.

Reasonable adjustment

What does the Act say about the duty of "reasonable adjustment"?

4.12 **The Act says** that the duty applies where any physical feature of premises occupied by the employer, or any arrangements made by or on behalf of the employer, cause a substantial disadvantage to a disabled person compared with non-disabled people. An employer has to take such steps as it is reasonable for him to have to take in all the circumstances to prevent that disadvantage – in other words the employer has to make a "reasonable adjustment" *(S6(1))*.

> A man who is disabled by dyslexia applies for a job which involves writing letters within fairly long deadlines. The employer gives all applicants a test of their letter-writing ability. The man can generally write letters very well but finds it difficult to do so in stressful situations. The *employer's arrangements* would mean he had to begin his test immediately on arrival and to do it in a short time. He would be *substantially disadvantaged compared to non-disabled people* who would not find such arrangements stressful or, if they did, would not be so affected by them. The employer therefore gives him a little time to settle in and longer to write the letter. These new arrangements do not inconvenience the employer very much and only briefly delay the decision on an appointment. These are *steps that it is reasonable for the employer to have to take in the circumstances to prevent the disadvantage* – a "reasonable adjustment".

4.13 If a disabled person cannot point to an existing non-disabled person compared with whom he is at a substantial disadvantage, then the comparison should be made with how the employer would have treated a non-disabled person.

4.14 How to comply with this duty in recruitment and during employment is explained in paragraphs 5.1–5.29 and 6.1–6.21. The following paragraphs explain how to satisfy this duty more generally.

What "physical features" and "arrangements" are covered by the duty?

4.15 **Regulations define** the term "physical features" to include anything on the premises arising from a building's design or construction or from an approach to, exit from or access to such a building; fixtures, fittings, furnishings, furniture, equipment or materials; and any other physical element or quality of land in the premises. All of these are covered whether temporary or permanent.[1]

4.16 **The Act says** that the duty applies to "arrangements" for determining to whom employment should be offered and any term, condition or arrangement on which employment, promotion, transfer, training or any other benefit is offered or afforded **(S6(2))**. The duty applies in recruitment and during employment; for example, selection and interview procedures and the arrangements for using premises for such procedures as well as job offers, contractual arrangements, and working conditions.

> The design of a particular workplace makes it difficult for someone with a hearing impairment to hear. That is a disadvantage caused by the *physical features*. There may be nothing that can reasonably be done in the circumstances to change these features. However, requiring someone to work in such a workplace is an *arrangement made by the employer* and it might be reasonable to overcome the disadvantage by a transfer to another workplace or by ensuring that the supervisor gives instructions in an office rather than in the working area.

What "disadvantages" give rise to the duty?

4.17 **The Act says** that only substantial disadvantages give rise to the duty **(S6(1))**. Substantial disadvantages are those which are not minor or trivial.

> An employer is unlikely to be required to widen a particular doorway to enable passage by an employee using a wheelchair if there is an easy alternative route to the same destination.

4.18 An employer cannot be required to prevent a disadvantage caused by premises or by non-pay arrangements by increasing the disabled person's pay. (See paragraph 5.29).

4.19 The duty of reasonable adjustment does not apply in relation to benefits under occupational pension schemes or certain benefits under other employment-related benefit schemes although there is a duty not to discriminate in relation to such benefits (see paragraphs 6.9–6.16).

1 Employment Regulations (see paragraph 1.6)

What adjustments might an employer have to make?

4.20 **The Act gives** a number of examples of "steps" which employers may have to take, if it is reasonable for them to have to do so in all the circumstances of the case **(S6(3))**. Steps other than those listed here, or a combination of steps, will sometimes have to be taken. The steps in the Act are:

■ *making adjustments to premises*

> An employer might have to make structural or other physical changes such as: widening a doorway, providing a ramp or moving furniture for a wheelchair user; relocating light switches, door handles or shelves for someone who has difficulty in reaching; providing appropriate contrast in decor to help the safe mobility of a visually impaired person.

■ *allocating some of the disabled person's duties to another person*

> Minor or subsidiary duties might be reallocated to another employee if the disabled person has difficulty in doing them because of the disability. For example, if a job occasionally involves going onto the open roof of a building an employer might have to transfer this work away from an employee whose disability involves severe vertigo.

■ *transferring the person to fill an existing vacancy*

> If an employee becomes disabled, or has a disability which worsens so she cannot work in the same place or under the same arrangements and there is no reasonable adjustment which would enable the employee to continue doing the current job, then she might have to be considered for any suitable alternative posts which are available. (Such a case might also involve reasonable retraining.)

■ *altering the person's working hours*

> This could include allowing the disabled person to work flexible hours to enable additional breaks to overcome fatigue arising from the disability, or changing the disabled person's hours to fit with the availability of a carer.

■ *assigning the person to a different place of work*

This could mean transferring a wheelchair user's work station from an inaccessible third floor office to an accessible one on the ground floor. It could mean moving the person to other premises of the same employer if the first building is inaccessible.

■ *allowing the person to be absent during working hours for rehabilitation, assessment or treatment*

For example, if a person were to become disabled, the employer might have to allow the person more time off during work, than would be allowed to non-disabled employees, to receive physiotherapy or psychoanalysis or undertake employment rehabilitation. A similar adjustment might be appropriate if a disability worsens or if a disabled person needs occasional treatment anyway.

■ *giving the person, or arranging for him to be given, training*

This could be training in the use of particular pieces of equipment unique to the disabled person, or training appropriate for all employees but which needs altering for the disabled person because of the disability. For example, all employees might need to be trained in the use of a particular machine but an employer might have to provide slightly different or longer training for an employee with restricted hand or arm movements,or training in additional software for a visually impaired person so that he can use a computer with speech output.

■ *acquiring or modifying equipment*

An employer might have to provide special equipment (such as an adapted keyboard for a visually impaired person or someone with arthritis), or an adapted telephone for someone with a hearing impairment or modified equipment (such as longer handles on a machine). There is no requirement to provide or modify equipment for personal purposes unconnected with work, such as providing a wheelchair if a person needs one in any event but does not have one: the disadvantage in such a case does not flow from the employer's arrangements or premises.

■ *modifying instructions or reference manuals*

The way instruction is normally given to employees might need to be revised when telling a disabled person how to do a task. The format of instructions or manuals may need to be modified (e.g. produced in braille or on audio tape) and instructions for people with learning disabilities may need to be conveyed orally with individual demonstration.

■ *modifying procedures for testing or assessment*

This could involve ensuring that particular tests do not adversely affect people with particular types of disability. For example, a person with restricted manual dexterity might be disadvantaged by a written test, so an employer might have to give that person an oral test.

■ *providing a reader or interpreter*

This could involve a colleague reading mail to a person with a visual impairment at particular times during the working day or, in appropriate circumstances, the hiring of a reader or sign language interpreter.

■ *providing supervision*

This could involve the provision of a support worker, or help from a colleague, in appropriate circumstances, for someone whose disability leads to uncertainty or lack of confidence.

When is it "reasonable" for an employer to have to make an adjustment?

4.21 Effective and practicable adjustments for disabled people often involve little or no cost or disruption and are therefore very likely to be reasonable for an employer to have to make. **The Act lists** a number of factors which may, in particular, have a bearing on whether it will be reasonable for the employer to have to make a particular adjustment **(S6(4))**. These factors make a useful checklist, particularly when considering more substantial adjustments. The effectiveness and practicability of a particular adjustment might be considered first. If it is practicable and effective, the financial aspects might be looked at as a whole – cost of the adjustment and resources available to fund it. Other factors might also have a bearing. The factors in the Act are listed below.

The effectiveness of the step in preventing the disadvantage

4.22 It is unlikely to be reasonable for an employer to have to make an adjustment involving little benefit to the disabled employee.

> A disabled person is significantly less productive than his colleagues and so is paid less. A particular adjustment would improve his output and thus his pay. It is more likely to be reasonable for the employer to have to make that adjustment if it would significantly improve his pay, than if the adjustment would make only a relatively small improvement.

The practicability of the step

4.23 It is more likely to be reasonable for an employer to have to take a step which is easy to take than one which is difficult.

> It might be impracticable for an employer who needs to appoint an employee urgently to have to wait for an adjustment to be made to an entrance. How long it might be reasonable for the employer to have to wait would depend on the circumstances. However, it might be possible to make a temporary adjustment in the meantime, such as using another, less convenient entrance.

The financial and other costs of the adjustment and the extent of any disruption caused

4.24 If an adjustment costs little or nothing and is not disruptive, it would be reasonable unless some other factor (such as practicability or effectiveness) made it unreasonable. The costs to be taken into account include staff and other resource costs. The significance of the cost of a step may depend in part on what the employer might otherwise spend in the circumstances.

> It would be reasonable for an employer to have to spend at least as much on an adjustment to enable the retention of a disabled person – including any retraining – as might be spent on recruiting and training a replacement.

4.25 The significance of the cost of a step may also depend in part on the value of the employee's experience and expertise to the employer.

Examples of the factors that might be considered as relating to the value of an employee would include:

- the amount of resources (such as training) invested in the individual by the employer;

- the employee's length of service;

- the employee's level of skill and knowledge;

- the employee's quality of relationships with clients;

- the level of the employee's pay.

4.26 It is more likely to be reasonable for an employer to have to make an adjustment with significant costs for an employee who is likely be in the job for some time than for a temporary employee.

4.27 An employer is more likely to have to make an adjustment which might cause only minor inconvenience to other employees or the employer than one which might unavoidably prevent other employees from doing their job, or cause other significant disruption.

The extent of the employer's financial or other resources

4.28 It is more likely to be reasonable for an employer with substantial financial resources to have to make an adjustment with a significant cost, than for an employer with fewer resources. The resources in practice available to the employer as a whole should be taken into account as well as other calls on those resources. The reasonableness of an adjustment will depend, however, not only on the resources in practice available for the adjustment but also on all other relevant factors (such as effectiveness and practicability).

4.29 Where the resources of the employer are spread across more than one "business unit" or "profit centre" the calls on them should also be taken into account in assessing reasonableness.

A large retailer probably could not show that the limited resources for which an individual shop manager is responsible meant it was not reasonable for the retailer to have to make an adjustment at that shop. Such an employer may, however, have a number – perhaps a large number – of other disabled employees in other shops. The employer's expenditure on other adjustments, or his potential expenditure on similar adjustments for other existing disabled employees, might then be taken into account in assessing the reasonableness of having to make a new adjustment for the disabled employee in question.

17

4.30 It is more likely to be reasonable for an employer with a substantial number of staff to have to make certain adjustments, than for a smaller employer.

> It would generally be reasonable for an employer with many staff to have to make significant efforts to reallocate duties, identify a suitable alternative post or provide supervision from existing staff. It could also be reasonable for a small company covered by the Act to have to make any of these adjustments but not if it involved disproportionate effort.

The availability to the employer of financial or other assistance to help make an adjustment.

4.31 The availability of outside help may well be a relevant factor.

> An employer, in recruiting a disabled person, finds that the only feasible adjustment is too costly for him alone. However, if assistance is available e.g. from a Government programme or voluntary body, it may well be reasonable for him to have to make the adjustment after all.

A disabled person is not required to contribute to the cost of a reasonable adjustment. However, if a disabled person has a particular piece of special or adapted equipment which he is prepared to use for work, this might make it reasonable for the employer to have to take some other step (as well as allowing use of the equipment).

> An employer requires his employees to use company cars for all business travel. One employee's disability means she would have to use an adapted car or an alternative form of transport. If she has an adapted car of her own which she is willing to use on business, it might well be reasonable for the employer to have to allow this and pay her an allowance to cover the cost of doing so, even if it would not have been reasonable for him to have to provide an adapted company car, or to pay an allowance to cover alternative travel arrangements in the absence of an adapted car.

Other factors

4.32 Although the Act does not mention any further factors, others might be relevant depending on the circumstances. For example:

- effect on other employees

Employees' adverse reaction to an adjustment being made for the disabled employee which involves something they too would like (such as a special working arrangement) is unlikely to be significant.

- adjustments made for other disabled employees

An employer may choose to give a particular disabled employee, or group of disabled employees, an adjustment which goes beyond the duty – that is, which is more than it is reasonable for him to have to do. This would not mean he necessarily had to provide a similar adjustment for other employees with a similar disability.

- the extent to which the disabled person is willing to cooperate

An employee with a mobility impairment works in a team located on an upper floor, to which there is no access by lift. Getting there is very tiring for the employee, and the employer could easily make a more accessible location available for him (though the whole team could not be relocated). If that was the only adjustment which it would be reasonable for the employer to have to make but the employee refused to work there then the employer would not have to make any adjustment at all.

Could an employer have to make more than one adjustment?

4.33 Yes, if it is reasonable for the employer to have to make more than one.

A woman who is deafblind is given a new job with her employer in an unfamiliar part of the building. The employer (i) arranges facilities for her guide dog in the new area, (ii) arranges for her new instructions to be in Braille and (iii) suggests to visitors ways in which they can communicate with her.

Does an employer have to justify not making an adjustment?

4.34 *The Act says* that it is discrimination if an employer fails to take a step which it is reasonable for him to have to take, and he cannot justify that failure *(S5(2))*. However, if it is unreasonable (under *S6*) for an employer to have to make any, or a particular, adjustment, he would not then also have to justify (under *S5*) not doing so. Failure to comply with the duty of reasonable adjustment can only be justified if the reason for the failure is material to the circumstances of the particular case and substantial *(S5(4))*.

> An employer might not make an adjustment which it was reasonable for him to have to make because of ignorance or wrong information about appropriate adjustments or about the availability of help with making an adjustment. He would then need to justify failing in his duty. It is unlikely that he could do so unless he had made a reasonable effort to obtain good information from a reputable source such as contacting the local Placing Assessment and Counselling Team or an appropriate disability organisation.

> If either of two possible adjustments would remove a disadvantage, but the employer has cost or operational reasons for preferring one rather than the other, it is unlikely to be reasonable for him to have to make the one that is not preferred. If, however, the employee refuses to cooperate with the proposed adjustment the employer is likely to be justified in not providing it.

> A disabled employee refuses to follow specific occupational medical advice provided on behalf of an employer about methods of working or managing his condition at work. If he has no good reason for this and his condition deteriorates as a result, the refusal may justify the employer's subsequent failure to make an adjustment for the worsened condition.

Building regulations, listed buildings, leases

How do building regulations affect reasonable adjustments?

4.35 A building or extension to a building may have been constructed in accordance with Part M of the building regulations (or the Scottish parallel, Part T of the Technical Standards) which is concerned with access and facilities for disabled people. *Regulations provide* in these circumstances that the employer does not have to alter any physical characteristic of the building or extension which still complies with the building regulations in force at the time the building works were carried out.[2]

2 Employment Regulations (see paragraph 1.6)

> Where the building regulations in force at the time of a building's construction required that a door should be a particular width, the employer would not have to alter the width of the door later. However, he might have to alter other aspects of the door (eg the type of handle).

4.36 Employers can only rely upon this defence if the feature still satisfies the requirement of the building regulations that applied when the building or extension was constructed.

What about the need to obtain statutory consent for some building changes?

4.37 Employers might have to obtain statutory consent before making adjustments involving changes to premises. Such consents include planning permission, listed building consent, scheduled monument consent and fire regulations approval. The Act does not override the need to obtain such consents *(S59)*. Therefore an employer does not have to make an adjustment if it requires a statutory consent which has not been given.

4.38 The time it would take to obtain consent may make a particular adjustment impracticable and therefore one which it is not reasonable for the employer to have to make. However, the employer would then also need to consider whether it was reasonable to have to make a temporary adjustment – one that does not require consent – in the meantime.

4.39 Employers should explore ways of making reasonable adjustments which either do not require statutory consent or are likely to receive it. They may well find it useful to consult their local planning authority (in England and Wales) or planning authority (in Scotland).

> An employer needs statutory consent to widen an internal doorway in a listed building for a woman disabled in an accident who returned to work in a wheelchair. The employer considers using a different office but this is not practicable. In the circumstances the widening would be a reasonable adjustment. The employer knows from the local planning authority that consent is likely to be given in a few weeks. In the meantime the employer arranges for the woman to share an accessible office which is inconvenient for both employees, but does not prevent them doing their jobs and is tolerable for that limited period.

What happens where a lease says that certain changes to premises cannot be made?

4.40 Special provisions apply where a lease would otherwise prevent a reasonable adjustment involving an alteration to premises. **The Act modifies** the effect of the lease so far as necessary to enable the employer to make the alteration if the landlord consents, and to provide that the landlord must not withhold consent unreasonably but may attach reasonable conditions to the consent **(S16)**.

How will arrangements for getting the landlord's consent work?

4.41 **The Act says** that the employer must write to the landlord (called the "lessor" in the Act) asking for consent to make the alteration. If an employer fails to apply to the landlord for consent, anything in the lease which would prevent that alteration must be ignored in deciding whether it was reasonable for the employer to have to make that alteration **(Sch4 Para 1)**. If the landlord consents, the employer can then carry out the alteration. If the landlord refuses consent the employer must notify the disabled person, but then has no further obligation.[3] Where the landlord fails to reply within 21 days or a reasonable period after that he is deemed to have withheld his consent. In those circumstances the withholding of the consent will be unreasonable (see paragraph 4.44).[4]

4.42 If the landlord attaches a condition to the consent and it is reasonable for the employer to have to carry out the alteration on that basis, the employer must then carry out the alteration. If it would not be reasonable for the employer to have to carry out the alteration on that basis, the employer must notify the disabled person, but then has no further obligation.

When is it unreasonable for a landlord to withhold consent?

4.43 This will depend on the circumstances but a trivial or arbitrary reason would almost certainly be unreasonable. Many reasonable adjustments to premises will not harm a landlord's interests and so it would generally be unreasonable to withhold consent for them.

> A particular adjustment helps make a public building more accessible generally and is therefore likely to benefit the landlord. It would very probably be unreasonable for consent to be withheld in these circumstances.

3 Employment Regulations (see paragraph 1.6)
4 Employment Regulations (see paragraph 1.6)

4.44 *Regulations provide* that withholding consent will be
unreasonable where:

- a landlord has failed to act within the time limits referred to in
paragraph 4.41 above (ie 21 days of receipt of the employer's
application or a reasonable period after that); or

- the lease says that consent will be given to alterations of that
type or says that such consent will be given if it is sought in a
particular way and it has been sought in that way.[5]

When is it reasonable for a landlord to withhold consent?

4.45 This will depend on the particular circumstances.

> A particular adjustment is likely to result in a substantial
> permanent reduction in the value of the landlord's interest in
> the premises. The landlord would almost certainly be acting
> reasonably in withholding consent.

> A particular adjustment would cause significant disruption or
> inconvenience to other tenants (for example, where the
> premises consist of multiple adjoining units). The landlord
> would be likely to be acting reasonably in withholding consent.

What conditions would it be reasonable for a landlord to make when giving consent?

4.46 This will depend on the particular circumstances. However,
Regulations provide that it would be reasonable for the landlord to
require the employer to meet any of the following conditions:

- obtain planning permission and other statutory consents;

- submit any plans to the landlord for approval (provided that the
landlord then confirms that approval will not be withheld
unreasonably);

- allow the landlord a reasonable opportunity to inspect the work
when completed;

- reimburse the landlord's reasonable costs incurred in connection
with the giving of his consent;

- reinstate the altered part of the premises to its former state
when the lease expires but only if it would have been reasonable
for the landlord to have refused consent in the first place.[6]

5 Employment Regulations (see paragraph 1.6)
6 Employment Regulations (see paragraph 1.6)

What happens if the landlord has a "superior" landlord?

4.47 The employer's landlord may also hold a lease which prevents him from consenting to the alteration without the consent of the "superior" landlord. The statutory provisions have been modified by regulations to cover this. The employer's landlord will be acting reasonably by notifying the employer that consent will be given if the superior landlord agrees. The employer's landlord must then apply to the superior landlord to ask for agreement. The provisions in paragraphs 4.41–4.46, including the requirements not to withhold consent unreasonably and not to attach unreasonable conditions, then apply to the superior landlord.[7]

What if some agreement other than a lease prevents the premises being altered?

4.48 An employer or landlord may be bound by the terms of an agreement or other legally binding obligation (for example, a mortgage or charge or restrictive covenant or, in Scotland, a feu disposition) under which the employer or landlord cannot alter the premises without someone else's consent. In these circumstances *Regulations provide* that it is always reasonable for the employer or landlord to have to take steps to obtain the necessary consent so that a reasonable adjustment can be made. Unless or until that consent is obtained the employer or landlord is not required to make the alteration in question. The step of seeking consent which it is always reasonable to have to take does not extend to having to apply to a court or tribunal.[8] Whether it is reasonable for the employer or landlord to have to apply to a court or tribunal would depend on the circumstances of the case.

Agreements which breach the Act's provisions

Can a disabled person waive rights, or an employer's duties, under the Act?

4.49 *The Act says* that any term in a contract of employment or other agreement is "void" (i.e. not valid) to the extent that it would require a person to do anything that would breach any of the Act's employment provisions, or exclude or limit the operation of those provisions *(S9)*.

4.50 An employer should not include in an agreement any provision intended to avoid obligations under the Act, or to prevent someone from fulfilling obligations. An agreement should not, therefore, be used to try to justify less favourable treatment or deem an adjustment unreasonable. Moreover, even parts of agreements which have such an effect (even

7   The Disability Discrimination (Sub-leases and Sub-tenancies) Regulations 1996
8   Employment Regulations (see paragraph 1.6)

though unintended) are made void if they would restrict the working of the employment provisions in the Act. However, special arrangements cover leases and other agreements which might prevent a change to premises which could be an adjustment under the Act but where the possible restrictions to the Act's working were unintentional. These are described in paragraphs 4.40–4.48.

4.51 The Act also says that a contract term is void if it would prevent anyone from making a claim under the employment provisions in an industrial tribunal *(S9)*. Further information is given in Annex 3 about such agreements.

What about permits issued in accordance with the Agricultural Wages Acts?

4.52 Under the Agricultural Wages Act 1948 and the Agricultural Wages (Scotland) Act 1949 minimum wages, and terms and conditions, can be set for agricultural workers. Permits can be issued to individuals who are "incapacitated" for the purposes of those Acts and they can then be paid such lower minimum rates or be subject to such revised terms and conditions of employment that the permit specifies. *Regulations provide* that the treatment of a disabled person in accordance with such a permit would be taken to be justified.[9] This would not prevent the employer from having to comply with the duty not to discriminate, including the duty of reasonable adjustment, for matters other than those covered by the permit.

Victimisation

What does the Act say about victimisation?

4.53 Victimisation is a special form of discrimination covered by the Act. *The Act makes* it unlawful for one person to treat another (the victim) less favourably than he would treat other people in the same circumstances because the "victim" has:

- brought, or given evidence or information in connection with, proceedings under the Act (whether or not proceedings are later withdrawn);

- done anything else under the Act; or

- alleged someone has contravened the Act (whether or not the allegation is later dropped);

9 Employment Regulations (see paragraph 1.6)

or because the person believes or suspects that the victim has done or intends to do any of these things *(S55)*.

It is unlawful for an employer to victimise either disabled or non-disabled people.

> A disabled employee complains of discrimination. It would be unlawful for the employer to subject non-disabled colleagues to any detriment (e.g. suspension) for telling the truth about the alleged discrimination at an industrial tribunal hearing or in any internal grievance procedures.

4.54 It is not victimisation to treat a person less favourably because that person has made an allegation which was false and not made in good faith *(S55(b))*.

(Harassment is covered in paragraphs 6.22–6.23.)

Setting up management systems to help avoid discrimination

What management systems might be set up to help avoid discrimination?

4.55 *The Act says* that employers are responsible for the actions done by their employees in the course of their employment. In legal proceedings against an employer based on actions of an employee, it is a defence that the employer took such steps as were reasonably practicable to prevent such actions. It is not a defence for the employer simply to show the action took place without his knowledge or approval. Employers who act through agents will also be liable for the actions of their agents done with the employer's express or implied authority *(S58)*.

> An employer makes it clear to a recruitment agency that the company will not take kindly to recruits with learning disabilities being put forward by the agency. The agency complies by not putting such candidates forward. Both the employer and the agency will be liable if such treatment cannot be justified in an individual case.

4.56 Employers should communicate to their employees and agents any policy they may have on disability matters, and any other policies which have elements relevant to disabled employees (such as health, absenteeism or equal opportunities). All staff should be made aware that it is unlawful to discriminate against disabled people, and be familiar with the policies and practices adopted by their employer to ensure compliance with the law. Employers should provide guidance on non-discriminatory practices for all employees, so they will be aware what they should do and how to deal with disabled colleagues and disabled applicants for vacancies in the organisation, and should ensure so far as possible that these policies and practices are implemented. Employers should also make it clear to their agents what is required of them with regard to their duties under the Act, and the extent of their authority.

4.57 *The Act says* that an employer is not under an obligation to make an adjustment if he does not know, and could not reasonably be expected to know, that a person has a disability which is likely to place the person at a substantial disadvantage *(S6(6))*. An employer must therefore do all he could reasonably be expected to do to find out whether this is the case.

> An employee has a disability which sometimes causes him to cry at work although the cause of this behaviour is not known to the employer. The employer's general approach on such matters is to tell staff to leave their personal problems at home and to make no allowance for such problems in the work arrangements. The employer disciplines the employee without giving him any opportunity to explain that the problem in fact arises from a disability. The employer would be unlikely to succeed in a claim that he could not reasonably be expected to have known of the disability or that it led to the behaviour for which the employee was disciplined.

> An employer has an annual appraisal system which specifically provides an opportunity to notify the employer in confidence if any employees are disabled and are put at a substantial disadvantage by the work arrangements or premises. This practice enables the employer to show that he could not reasonably be expected to know that an employee was put at such a disadvantage as a result of disability, if this was not obvious and was not brought to the employer's attention through the appraisal system.

4.58 In some cases a reasonable adjustment will not work without the co-operation of other employees. Employees may therefore have an important role in helping to ensure that a reasonable adjustment is carried out in practice.

> It is a reasonable adjustment for an employer to communicate in a particular way to an employee with autism (a disability which can make it difficult for someone to understand normal social interaction among people). As part of the reasonable adjustment it is the responsibility of that employer to seek the co-operation of other employees in communicating in that way.

4.59 It may be necessary to tell one or more of a disabled person's colleagues (in confidence) about a disability which is not obvious and/or whether any special assistance is required. This may be limited to the person's supervisor, or it may be necessary to involve other colleagues, depending on the nature of the disability and the reason they need to know about it.

> In order for a person with epilepsy to work safely in a particular factory, it may be necessary to advise fellow workers about the effects of the condition, and the methods for assisting with them.

> An office worker with cancer says that he does not want colleagues to know of his condition. As an adjustment he needs extra time away from work to receive treatment and to rest. Neither his colleagues nor the line manager needs to be told the precise reasons for the extra leave but the latter will need to know that the adjustment is required in order to carry it out effectively.

4.60 The extent to which an employer is entitled to let other staff know about an employee's disability will depend at least in part on the terms of employment. An employer could be held to be discriminating in revealing such information about a disabled employee if the employer would not reveal similar information about another person for an equally legitimate management purpose; or if the employer revealed such information without consulting the individual, whereas the employer's usual practice would be to talk to an employee before revealing personal information about him.

4.61 The Act does not prevent a disabled person keeping a disability confidential from an employer. But this is likely to mean that unless the employer could reasonably be expected to know about the person's disability anyway, the employer will not be under a duty to make a reasonable adjustment. If a disabled person expects an employer to make a reasonable adjustment, he will need to provide the employer – or, as the case may be, someone acting on the employer's behalf – with sufficient information to carry out that adjustment.

> An employee has symptomatic HIV. He prefers not to tell his employer of the condition. However, as the condition progresses, he finds it increasingly difficult to work the required number of hours in a week. Until he tells his employer of his condition – or the employer becomes or could reasonably be expected to be aware of it – he cannot require the employer to change his working hours to overcome the difficulty. However, once the employer is informed he may then have to make a reasonable adjustment.

4.62 If an employer's agent or employee (for example, an occupational health officer, a personnel officer or line manager) knows in that capacity of an employee's disability, then the employer cannot claim that he does not know of that person's disability, and that he is therefore excluded from the obligation to make a reasonable adjustment. This will be the case even if the disabled person specifically asked for such information to be kept confidential. Employers will therefore need to ensure that where information about disabled people may come through different channels, there is a means – suitably confidential – for bringing the information together, so the employer's duties under the Act are fulfilled.

> In a large company an occupational health officer is engaged by the employer to provide him with information about his employees' health. The officer becomes aware of an employee's disability, which the employee's line manager does not know about. The employer's working arrangements put the employee at a substantial disadvantage because of the effects of her disability and she claims that a reasonable adjustment should have been made. It will not be a defence for the employer to claim that he did not know of her disability. This is because the information gained by the officer on the employer's behalf is imputed to the employer. Even if the person did not want the line manager to know that she had a disability, the occupational health officer's knowledge means that the employer's duty under the Act applies. It might even be necessary for the line manager to implement reasonable adjustments without knowing precisely why he has to do so.

4.63 Information will not be imputed to the employer if it is gained by a person providing services to employees independently of the employer. This is the case even if the employer has arranged for those services to be provided.

An employer contracts with an agency to provide an independent counselling service to employees. The contract says that the counsellors are not acting on the employer's behalf while in the counselling role. Any information about a person's disability obtained by a counsellor during such counselling would not be imputed to the employer and so could not itself place a duty of reasonable adjustment on the employer.

What if someone says they have a disability and the employer is not convinced?

4.64 If a candidate asks for an adjustment to be made because of an impairment whose effects are not obvious, nothing in the Act or Regulations would prohibit the employer from asking for evidence that the impairment is one which gives rise to a disability as defined in the Act.

An applicant says she has a mental illness whose effects require her to take time off work on a frequent, but irregular, basis. If not satisfied that this is true, the employer would be entitled to ask for evidence that the woman has a mental illness which was likely to have the effects claimed and that it is clinically well recognised (as required by the Act).

Effects of other legislation

What about the effects of other legislation?

4.65 An employer is not required to make an adjustment – or do anything under the Act – that would result in a breach of statutory obligations *(S59)*.

If a particular adjustment would breach health and safety or fire legislation then an employer would not have to make it. However, the employer would still have to consider whether he was required to make any other adjustment which would not breach any legislation. For instance, if someone in a wheelchair could not use emergency evacuation arrangements such as a fire escape on a particular floor, it might be reasonable for the employer to have to relocate that person's job to an office where that problem did not arise.

An employer shortlisting applicants to fill a junior office post is considering whether to include a blind applicant who the employer believes might present a safety risk moving around the crowded office. A reasonable adjustment might be to provide mobility training to familiarise the applicant with the work area, so removing any risk there might otherwise be.

What about legislation which places restrictions on what employers can do to recruit disabled people?

4.66 The Disability Discrimination Act does not prevent posts being advertised as open only to disabled candidates. However, the requirement, for example, under Section 7 of the Local Government and Housing Act 1989 that every appointment to local authorities must be made on merit means that a post cannot be so advertised. Applications from disabled people can nevertheless be encouraged. However, this requirement to appoint "on merit" does not exclude the duty under the 1995 Act to make adjustments so a disabled person's "merit" must be assessed taking into account any such adjustments which would have to be made.

Discrimination against applicants

How does the Act affect recruitment?

5.1 *The Act says* that it is unlawful for an employer to discriminate against a disabled person:

- in the arrangements made for determining who should be offered employment;

- in the terms on which the disabled person is offered employment; or

- by refusing to offer, or deliberately not offering, the disabled person employment *S4(1)*.

5.2 The word "arrangements" has a wide meaning. Employers should avoid discrimination in, for example, specifying the job, advertising the job, and the processes of selection, including the location and timing of interviews, assessment techniques, interviewing, and selection criteria.

Specifying the job

Does the Act affect how an employer should draw up a job specification?

5.3 Yes. The inclusion of unnecessary or marginal requirements in a job specification can lead to discrimination.

> An employer stipulates that employees must be "energetic", when in fact the job in question is largely sedentary in nature. This requirement could unjustifiably exclude some people whose disabilities result in them getting tired more easily than others.

> An employer specifies that a driving licence is required for a job which involves limited travelling. An applicant for the job has no driving licence because of the particular effects in his case of cerebral palsy. He is otherwise the best candidate for that job, he could easily and cheaply do the travelling involved other than by driving and it would be a reasonable adjustment for the employer to let him do so. It would be discriminatory to insist on the specification and reject his application solely because he had no driving licence.

5.4   Blanket exclusions (i.e. exclusions which do not take account of individual circumstances) may lead to discrimination.

> An employer excludes people with epilepsy from all driving jobs. One of the jobs, in practice, only requires a standard licence and normal insurance cover. If, as a result, someone with epilepsy, who has such a licence and can obtain such cover, is turned down for the job then the employer will probably have discriminated unlawfully in excluding her from consideration.

> An employer stipulates that candidates for a job must not have a history of mental illness, believing that such candidates will have poor attendance. The employer rejects an applicant solely because he has had a mental illness without checking the individual's probable attendance. Even if good attendance is genuinely essential for the job, this is not likely to be justified and is therefore very likely to be unlawful discrimination.

Can an employer stipulate essential health requirements?

5.5   Yes, but the employer may need to justify doing so, and to show that it would not be reasonable for him to have to waive them, in any individual case.

Can employers simply prefer a certain type of person?

5.6   Stating that a certain personal, medical or health-related characteristic is desirable may also lead to discrimination if the characteristic is not necessary for the performance of the job. Like a requirement, a preference may be decisive against an otherwise well-qualified disabled candidate and may have to be justified in an individual case.

> An employer prefers all employees to have a certain level of educational qualification. A woman with a learning disability, which has prevented her from obtaining the preferred qualification, is turned down for a job because she does not have that qualification. If the qualification is not necessary in order to do the job and she is otherwise the best candidate, then the employer will have discriminated unlawfully against her.

Publicising the vacancy

What does the Act say about how an employer can advertise vacancies?

5.7   Where a job is advertised, and a disabled person who applies is refused or deliberately not offered it and complains to an industrial tribunal about disability discrimination, the Act requires the tribunal to assume (unless the employer can prove otherwise) that the reason the person did not get the job was related to his disability if the advertisement could reasonably be taken to indicate:

- that the success of a person's application for the job might depend to any extent on the absence of a disability such as the applicant's; or

- that the employer is unwilling to make an adjustment for a disabled person **(S11)**.

> An employer puts in an advertisement for an office worker, "Sorry, but gaining access to our building can be difficult for some people". A man, who as a result of an accident some years previously can only walk with the aid of crutches but can do office work, applies for the job and is turned down. He complains to an industrial tribunal. Because of the wording of the advertisement, the tribunal would have to assume that he did not get the job for a reason relating to his disability unless the employer could prove otherwise.

What is an "advertisement" for the purposes of the Act?

5.8   *According to the Act* "advertisement" includes every form of advertisement or notice, whether to the public or not **(S11(3))**. This would include advertisements internal to a company or office.

Does an employer have to provide information about jobs in alternative formats?

5.9   In particular cases, this may be a reasonable adjustment.

> A person whom the employer knows to be disabled asks to be given information about a job in a medium that is accessible to her (in large print, in braille, on tape or on computer disc). It is often likely to be a reasonable adjustment for the employer to comply, particularly if the employer's information systems, and the time available before the new employee is needed, mean it can easily be done.

Can an employer say that he would welcome applications from disabled people?

5.10 Yes. *The Act does not prevent* this and it would be a positive and public statement of the employer's policy.

Can an employer include a question on an application form asking whether someone is disabled?

5.11 Yes. *The Act does not prevent* employers including such a question on application forms. Employers can also ask whether the individual might need an adjustment and what it might be.

Selection

Does the duty of reasonable adjustment apply to applicants?

5.12 *The Act says* that the duty to make a reasonable adjustment does not apply where the employer does not know, and could not reasonably be expected to know, that the disabled person in question is or may be an applicant for the post, or, that a particular applicant has a disability which is likely to place him at a disadvantage *(S6(a))*.

Does an employer have to take special care when considering applications?

5.13 Yes. Employers and their staff or agents must not discriminate against disabled people in the way in which they deal with applications. They may also have to make reasonable adjustments.

> Because of his disability, a candidate asks to submit an application in a particular medium, different from that specified for candidates in general (e.g. typewritten, by telephone, or on tape). It would normally be a reasonable adjustment for the employer to allow this.

Whom can an employer shortlist for interview?

5.14 If an employer knows that an applicant has a disability and is likely to be at a substantial disadvantage because of the employer's arrangements or premises, the employer should consider whether there is any reasonable adjustment which would bring the disabled person within the field of applicants to be considered even though he would not otherwise be within that field because of that disadvantage. If the employer could only make this judgement with more information it would be discriminatory for him not to put the disabled person on the shortlist for interview if that is how he would normally seek additional information about candidates.

What should an employer do when arranging interviews?

5.15 Employers should think ahead for interviews. Giving applicants the opportunity to indicate any relevant effects of a disability and to suggest adjustments to help overcome any disadvantage the disability may cause, could help the employer avoid discrimination in the interview and in considering the applicant, by clarifying whether any reasonable adjustments may be required.

5.16 Nevertheless, if a person, whom the employer previously did not know, and could not have known, to be disabled, arrives for interview and is placed at a substantial disadvantage because of the arrangements, the employer may still be under a duty to make a reasonable adjustment from the time that he first learns of the disability and the disadvantage. However, what the employer has to do in such circumstances might be less extensive than if advance notice had been given.

What changes might an employer have to make to arrangements for interviews?

5.17 There are many possible reasonable adjustments, depending on the circumstances.

> A person has difficulty attending at a particular time because of a disability. It will very likely be reasonable for the employer to have to rearrange the time.

> A hearing impaired candidate has substantial difficulties with the interview arrangements. The interviewer may simply need to ensure he faces the applicant and speaks clearly or is prepared to repeat questions. The interviewer should make sure that his face is well lit when talking to someone with a hearing or visual impairment. It will almost always be reasonable for an employer to have to provide such help with communication support if the interviewee would otherwise be at a substantial disadvantage.

An employer who pays expenses to candidates who come for interview could well have to pay additional expenses to meet any special requirements of a disabled person arising from any substantial disadvantage to which she would otherwise be put by the interview arrangements. This might include paying travelling expenses for a support worker or reasonable cost of travel by taxi, rather than by bus or train, if this is necessary because of the disability.

A job applicant does not tell an employer (who has no knowledge of her disability) in advance that she uses a wheelchair. On arriving for the interview she discovers that the room is not accessible. The employer did not know of the disability and so could not have been expected to make changes in advance. However, it would still be a reasonable adjustment for the employer to hold the interview in an alternative accessible room, if a suitable one was easily available at the time with no, or only an acceptable level of, disruption or additional cost.

Should an employer consider making changes to the way the interview is carried out?

5.18 Yes, although whether any change is needed – and, if so, what change – will depend on the circumstances.

It would almost always be reasonable to allow an applicant with a learning disability to bring a supportive person such as a friend or relative to assist when answering questions that are not part of tests.

It would normally be reasonable to allow a longer time for an interview to someone with a hearing impairment using a sign language interpreter to communicate.

Does an employer have to make changes to anticipate *any* disabled person applying for a job?

5.19 No. An employer is not required to make changes in anticipation of applications from disabled people in general. It is only if the employer knows or could be reasonably expected to know that a particular disabled person is, or may be, applying and is likely to be substantially disadvantaged by the employer's premises or arrangements, that the employer may have to make changes.

Should an employer ask about a disability?

5.20 The Act does not prohibit an employer from seeking information about a disability but an employer must not use it to discriminate against a disabled person. An employer should ask only about a disability if it is, or may be, relevant to the person's ability to do the job – after a reasonable adjustment, if necessary. Asking about the effects of a disability might be important in deciding what adjustments ought to be made. The employer should avoid discriminatory questions.

> An applicant whose disability has left him using a wheelchair but healthy, is asked by an employer whether any extra leave might be required because of the condition. This is unlikely to be discriminatory because a need for extra time off work may be a substantial factor relevant to the person's ability to do the job. Therefore such a question would normally be justified. Similarly, a reasonable question about whether any changes may need to be made to the workplace to accommodate the use of the wheelchair would probably not be discriminatory.

Does the Act prevent employers carrying out aptitude or other tests in the recruitment process?

5.21 No, but routine testing of all candidates may still discriminate against particular individuals or substantially disadvantage them. If so, the employer would need to revise the tests – or the way the results of such tests are assessed – to take account of specific disabled candidates, except where the nature and form of the test were necessary to assess a matter relevant to the job. It may, for instance, be a reasonable adjustment to accept a lower "pass rate" for a person whose disability inhibits performance in such a test. The extent to which this is required would depend on how closely the test is related to the job in question and what adjustments the employer might have to make if the applicant were given the job.

> An employer sets a numeracy test for prospective employees. A person with a learning disability takes the test and does not achieve the level the employer normally stipulates. If the job in fact entails very little numerical work and the candidate is otherwise well suited for the job it is likely to be a reasonable adjustment for the employer to waive the requirement.

An employer sets candidates a short oral test. An applicant is disabled by a bad stammer, but only under stress. It may be a reasonable adjustment to allow her more time to complete the test, or to give the test in written form instead, though not if oral communication is relevant to the job and assessing this was the purpose of the test.

Can an employer specify qualifications?

5.22 An employer is entitled to specify that applicants for a job must have certain qualifications. However, if a disabled person is rejected for the job because he lacks a qualification, the employer will have to justify that rejection if the reason why the person is rejected (i.e. the lack of a qualification) is connected with his disability. Justification will involve showing that the qualification is relevant and significant in terms of the particular job and the particular applicant, and that there is no reasonable adjustment which would change this. In some circumstances it might be feasible to reassign those duties to which the qualification relates, or to waive the requirement for the qualification if this particular applicant has alternative evidence of the necessary level of competence.

An employer seeking someone to work in an administrative post specifies that candidates must have the relevant NVQ Level 4 qualification. If Level 4 fairly reflects the complex and varied nature and substantial personal responsibility of the work, and these aspects of the job cannot reasonably be altered, the employer will be able to justify rejecting a disabled applicant who has only been able to reach Level 3 because of his disability and who cannot show the relevant level of competence by other means.

An employer specifies that two GCSEs are required for a certain post. This is to show that a candidate has the general level of ability required. No particular subjects are specified. An applicant whose dyslexia prevented her from passing written examinations cannot meet this requirement, but the employer would be unable to justify rejecting her on this account alone if she could show she nevertheless had the skill and intelligence called for in the post.

Can an employer insist on a disabled person having a medical examination?

5.23 Yes. However, if an employer insists on a medical check for a disabled person and not others, without justification, he will probably be discriminating unlawfully. The fact that a person has a disability is unlikely in itself to justify singling out that person to have a health check, although such action might be justified in relation to some jobs

An employer requires all candidates for employment to have a medical examination. That employer would normally be entitled to include a disabled person.

An applicant for a job has a disabling heart condition. The employer routinely issues a health questionnaire to job applicants, and requires all applicants who state they have a disability to undergo a medical examination. Under the Act, the employer would not be justified in requiring a medical examination whenever an applicant states he has a disability – for example, this would not normally be justified if the disability is clearly relevant neither to the job nor to the environment in which the job is done. However, the employer would probably be justified in asking the applicant with the disabling heart condition to have a medical examination restricted to assessing its implications for the particular job in its context. If, for example, the job required lifting and carrying but these abilities were limited by the condition, the employer would also have to consider whether it would be reasonable for him to have to make a change such as providing a mechanical means of lifting and/or carrying, or arranging for the few items above the person's limit to be dealt with by another person, whilst ensuring that any health and safety provisions were not breached.

How can an employer take account of medical evidence?

5.24 In most cases, having a disability does not adversely affect a person's general health. Medical evidence about a disability can justify an adverse employment decision (such as dismissing or not promoting). It will not generally do so if there is no effect on the person's ability to do the work (or any effect is less than substantial), however great the effects of the disability are in other ways. The condition or effects must be relevant to the employer's decision.

An applicant for a post on a short-term contract has a progressive condition which has some effects, but is likely to have substantial adverse effects only in the long term. The likelihood of these long-term effects would not itself be a justifiable reason for the employer to reject him.

An employer requires all candidates for a certain job to be able to work for at least two years to complete a particular work project. Medical evidence shows that a particular candidate is unlikely to be able to continue working for that long. It would be lawful to reject that candidate if the two-year requirement was justified in terms of the work, and if it would not be reasonable for the employer to have to waive it in the particular circumstances.

Advice from an occupational health expert simply that an employee was "unfit for work" would not mean that the employer's duty to make a reasonable adjustment was waived.

What will help an employer decide to select a particular disabled person?

5.25 The employer must take into account any adjustments that it is reasonable for him to have to make. Suggestions made by the candidate at any stage may assist in identifying these.

What if a disabled person just isn't the right person for the job?

5.26 An employer must not discriminate against a disabled candidate, but there is no requirement (aside from reasonable adjustment) to treat a disabled person more favourably than he treats or would treat others. An employer will have to assess an applicant's merits as they would be if any reasonable adjustments required under the Act had been made. If, after allowing for those adjustments, a disabled person would not be the best person for the job the employer would not have to recruit that person.

Terms and conditions of service

Are there restrictions on the terms and conditions an employer can offer a disabled person?

5.27 Terms and conditions of service should not discriminate against a disabled person. The employer should consider whether any reasonable adjustments need to be made to the terms and conditions which would otherwise apply.

> An employer's terms and conditions state the hours an employee has to be in work. It might be a reasonable adjustment to change these hours for someone whose disability means that she has difficulty using public transport during rush hours.

Does that mean that an employer can never offer a disabled person a less favourable contract?

5.28 No. Such a contract may be justified if there is a material and substantial reason and there is no reasonable adjustment which can be made to remove that reason.

> A person's disability means she has significantly lower output than other employees doing similar work, even after an adjustment. Her work is of neither lower nor higher quality than theirs. The employer would be justified in paying her less in proportion to the lower output if it affected the value of her work to the business.

Can employers still operate performance-related pay?

5.29 *Regulations provide* that this is justified so long as the scheme applies equally to all employees, or all of a particular class of employees. There would be no requirement to make a reasonable adjustment to an arrangement of this kind to ensure (for example) that a person's pay was topped up if a deteriorating condition happened to lead to lower performance.[10] However, there would still be a duty to make a reasonable adjustment to any aspect of the premises or work arrangements if that would prevent the disability reducing the employee's performance.

10 Employment Regulations (see paragraph 1.6)

Employment

Discrimination against employees

Does the Act cover all areas of employment?

6.1   Yes. *The Act* says that it is unlawful for an employer to discriminate against a disabled person whom he employs:

- in the terms of employment which he affords him;

- in the opportunities which he affords him for promotion, a transfer, training or receiving any other benefit;

- by refusing to afford him, or deliberately not affording him, any such opportunity; or

- by dismissing him, or subjecting him to any other detriment *(S4(2))*.

6.2 Therefore, an employer should not discriminate in relation to, for example: terms and conditions of service, arrangements made for induction, arrangements made for employees who become disabled (or who have a disability which worsens), opportunities for promotion, transfer, training or receiving any other benefit, or refusal of such opportunities, pensions, dismissal or any detriment.

Induction

What is the effect on induction procedures?

6.3   Employers must not discriminate in their induction procedures. The employer may have to make adjustments to ensure a disabled person is introduced into a new working environment in a clearly structured and supported way with, if necessary, an individually tailored induction programme *(S4(2) and S6(1))*.

> An employer runs a one day induction course for new recruits. A recruit with a learning disability is put at a substantial disadvantage by the way the course is normally run. The employer might have to make an alternative arrangement: for example running a separate, longer course for the person, or permitting someone to sit in on the normal course to provide support, assistance or encouragement.

Promotion and transfer

What are an employer's duties as far as promotion and transfer are concerned?

6.4   Employers must not discriminate in assessing a disabled person's suitability for promotion or transfer, in the practical arrangements necessary to enable the promotion or transfer to take place, in the operation of the appraisal, selection and promotion or transfer process, or in the new job itself – and may have to make a reasonable adjustment *(S4(2)(b) and (c) and S6(1))*.

> A garage owner does not consider for promotion to assistant manager a clerk who has lost the use of her right arm, because he wrongly and unreasonably believes that her disability might prevent her performing competently in a managerial post. The reason used by the employer to deny the clerk promotion has meant that she was discriminated against.

> An employer considering a number of people for a job on promotion is aware that one of the candidates for interview has a hearing impairment, but does not find out whether the person needs any special arrangements for the interview, for example a sign language interpreter. If the candidate requires such an adjustment, and it would be reasonable for the employer to have to make it, the employer would fail in his duty if he did not make that adjustment.

> A civil engineer whose disability involves kidney dialysis treatment, is based in London and regularly visits hospital for the treatment. She wishes to transfer to a vacant post in her company's Scottish office. She meets all the requirements for the post, but her transfer is turned down on the ground that her need for treatment would mean that, away from the facilities in London, she would be absent from work for longer. The employer had made no attempt to discuss this with her or get medical advice. If the employer had done so, it would have been clear that similar treatment would be equally available in the new locality. In these circumstances, the employer probably could not show that relying on this reason was justified.

Someone disabled by a back injury is seeking promotion to supervisor. A minor duty involves assisting with the unloading of the weekly delivery van, which the person's back injury would prevent. In assessing her suitability for promotion, the employer should consider whether reallocating this duty to another person would be a reasonable adjustment.

What should an employer do to check that promotion and transfer arrangements do not discriminate?

6.5   The employer should review the arrangements to check that qualifications required are justified for the job to be done. He should also check that other arrangements, for example systems which determine other criteria for a particular job, do not exclude disabled people who may have been unable to meet those criteria because of their disability but would be capable of performing well in the job.

Training and other benefits provided by the employer

Does the Act apply to the provision of training?

6.6   Yes. Employers must not discriminate in selection for training and must make any necessary reasonable adjustments *(S4(2)(b) and (c) and S6(1))*.

An employer wrongly assumes that a disabled person will be unwilling or unable to undertake demanding training or attend a residential training course, instead of taking an informed decision. He may well not be able to justify a decision based on that assumption.

An employer may need to alter the time or the location of the training for someone with a mobility problem, make training manuals, slides or other visual media accessible to a visually impaired employee, perhaps by providing braille versions or having them read out, or ensure that an induction loop is available for someone with a hearing impairment.

> An employer refuses to allow a disabled employee to be coached for a theory examination relating to practical work which the disability prevented the employee from doing. The employer would almost always be justified in refusing to allow the coaching because it was designed to equip employees for an area of work for which, because of the disability, the person could not be suited even by a reasonable adjustment.

What about other benefits provided by employers?

6.7   An employer must not discriminate in providing disabled people with opportunities for receiving benefits (which include "facilities" and "services") which are available to other employees *(S4(2)(b) and (c))*. The employer must make any necessary reasonable adjustment to the way the benefits are provided *(S6(1))* although this does not apply to benefits under occupational pension schemes or certain other employment related benefit schemes (paragraph 6.16).

> Benefits might include canteens, meal vouchers, social clubs and other recreational activities, dedicated car parking spaces, discounts on products, bonuses, share options, hairdressing, clothes allowances, financial services, healthcare, medical assistance/insurance, transport to work, company car, education assistance, workplace nurseries, and rights to special leave.

> If physical features of a company's social club would inhibit a disabled person's access it might be a reasonable adjustment for the employer to make suitable modifications.

> An employer provides dedicated car parking spaces near to the workplace. It is likely to be reasonable for the employer to have to allocate one of these spaces to a disabled employee who has significant difficulty getting from the public car parks further away that he would otherwise have to use.

6.8   If an employer provides benefits to the public, or to a section of the public which includes the disabled employee, provision of those benefits will normally fall outside the duty not to discriminate in employment. Instead, the duty in the Act not to discriminate in providing goods, facilities and services will apply. However, the employment duty will apply if the benefit to employees is materially different (eg. at a discount), is governed by the contract of employment, or relates to training *(S4(2) and (3))*.

A disabled employee of a supermarket chain who believes he has been discriminated against when buying goods as a customer at any branch of the supermarket would have no claim under the employment provisions. However, if that employee were using a discount card provided only to employees, then the employment provisions would apply if any less favourable treatment related to his use of the card.

Occupational pension schemes and insurance

What does the Act say about occupational pension schemes?

6.9 *The Act inserts* into every scheme a "non-discrimination" rule. The trustees or managers of the scheme are prohibited by that rule from doing – or omitting to do – anything to members or non-members of schemes that would be unlawful discrimination if done by an employer *(S17)*. References to employers in paragraphs 6.11–6.15 should therefore be read as if they also apply to trustees or managers when appropriate.

When is less favourable treatment justified?

6.10 Less favourable treatment for a reason relating to a disability can be justified only if the reason is material and substantial.

Trustees of a pension scheme would not be justified in excluding a woman simply because she had a visual impairment. That fact, in itself, would be no reason why she should not receive the same pension benefits as any other employee.

6.11 There are circumstances when a disabled person's health or health prognosis is such that the cost of providing benefits under a pension scheme is substantially greater than it would be for a person without the disability. In these circumstances *Regulations provide* that an employer is regarded as justified in treating a disabled person less favourably in applying the eligibility conditions for receiving the benefit. Employers should satisfy themselves, if necessary with actuarial advice and/or medical evidence, of the likelihood of there being a substantially greater cost.[11]

When could the justification be used?

6.12 The justification would be available whenever the disabled person is considered for admission to the scheme. However, the justification cannot be applied to a disabled member, unless a term was imposed at the time of admission which allowed this.

11 Employment Regulations (see paragraph 1.6)

Which benefits does this justification apply to?

6.13 The justification can apply to the following types of benefits provided by an occupational pension scheme: termination of service, retirement, old age or death, accident, injury, sickness or invalidity.[12]

Would a minor degree of extra cost amount to a justification for less favourable treatment?

6.14 No. Only the likelihood of a substantial additional cost should be taken to be a justification. Substantial means something more than minor or trivial.[13]

> An employer receives medical advice that an individual with multiple sclerosis is likely to retire early on health grounds. The employer obtains actuarial advice that the cost of providing that early retirement benefit would be substantially greater than an employee without MS and so the individual is refused access to the scheme. This is justified.

What happens to an employee's rate of contributions if the employer is justified in refusing the employee access to some benefits but not others?

6.15 *Regulations provide* that if the employer sets a uniform rate of contribution the employer would be justified in applying it to a disabled person. A disabled person could therefore be required to pay the same rate of contributions as other employees, even if not eligible for some of the benefits.[14]

Does the duty to make a reasonable adjustment apply?

6.16 No. The duty of reasonable adjustment does not apply to the provision of benefits under an occupational pension scheme or any other benefit payable in money or money's worth under a scheme or arrangement for the benefit of employees in respect of:

- ■ termination of service;

- ■ retirement, old age or death; or

- ■ accident, injury, sickness or invalidity *(S6(11))*. (Although there is power to add other matters to this list by regulations, none have been added at the date of this Code).

12 Employment Regulations (see paragraph 1.6)
13 Employment Regulations (see paragraph 1.6)
14 Employment Regulations (see paragraph 1.6)

Therefore, neither the employer nor the scheme's trustees or managers need to make any adjustment for a disabled person who, without that adjustment, will be justifiably denied access either to such a scheme or to a benefit under the scheme. Nor will they have to make an adjustment for someone receiving less benefit because they justifiably receive a lower rate of pay.

Does the Act cover the provision of insurance schemes for individual employees?

6.17 The Act also applies to provision of group insurance, such as permanent health insurance or life insurance, by an insurance company for employees under an arrangement with their employer. A disabled person in, or who applies or is considering applying to join, a group of employees covered by such an arrangement is protected from discrimination in the provision of the insurance services in the same way as if he were a member of the public seeking the services of that insurance company under the part of the Act relating to the provision of goods, facilities and services. However, the right of redress in this case would be exercised through an industrial tribunal (and not the courts) *(S18)*.

Does the Act cover the provision of insurance to an employer?

6.18 The employer may have to make reasonable adjustments to remove any disadvantage caused to a disabled person which arose from the arrangements made by the employer to provide himself with insurance cover. Such adjustments could include measures which would reduce any risk otherwise posed by the disabled person, so that the insurer would then provide cover, or seeking alternative cover. If cover could not be obtained at all at realistic cost it is most unlikely that the employer would have to bear the risk himself.

It comes to an employer's attention that someone who works for his antiques business has epilepsy. The employer is obliged to notify his insurance company who refuse to cover the employer against damage caused by the disabled person. To avoid dismissing the employee, it might be reasonable for the employer to have to bar the person from contact with valuable items, if this would mean the insurance company then provided cover.

Retention of disabled employees

6.19 An employer must not discriminate against an employee who becomes disabled, or has a disability which worsens *(S4(2))*. The issue of retention might also arise when an employee has a stable impairment but the nature of his employment changes.

6.20 If as a result of the disability an employer's arrangements or a physical feature of the employer's premises place the employee at a substantial disadvantage in doing his existing job, the employer must first consider any reasonable adjustment that would resolve the difficulty. The employer may also need to consult the disabled person at appropriate stages about what his needs are and what effect the disability might have on future employment, for example, where the employee has a progressive condition. The nature of the reasonable adjustments which an employer may have to consider will depend on the circumstances of the case.

It may be possible to modify a job to accommodate an employee's changed needs. This might be by rearranging working methods or giving another employee certain minor tasks the newly disabled person can no longer do, providing practical aids or adaptations to premises or equipment, or allowing the disabled person to work at different times or places from those with equivalent jobs (for instance, it may be that a change to part-time work might be appropriate for someone who needed to spend some time each week having medical treatment).

A newly disabled employee is likely to need time to readjust. For example, an employer might allow: a trial period to assess whether the employee is able to cope with the current job, or a new one; the employee initially to work from home; a gradual build-up to full time hours; or additional training for a person with learning disabilities who moves to another workplace.

It may be a reasonable adjustment for an employer to move a newly disabled person to a different post within the organisation if a suitable vacancy exists or is expected shortly.

Additional job coaching may be necessary to enable a disabled person to take on a new job.

In many cases where no reasonable adjustment would overcome a particular disability so as to enable the disabled person to continue with similar terms or conditions, it might be reasonable for the employer to have to offer a disabled employee a lower-paying job, applying the rate of pay that would apply to such a position under his usual pay practices.

If new technology (for instance a telephone or information technology system) puts a disabled person at a substantial disadvantage compared with non-disabled people, then the employer would be under a duty to make a reasonable adjustment. For example, some telephone systems may interfere with hearing aids for people with hearing impairments and the quality of the inductive coupler may need to be improved.

Termination of employment

6.21 Dismissal – including compulsory early retirement – of a disabled person for a reason relating to the disability would need to be justified and the reason for it would have to be one which could not be removed by any reasonable adjustment.

It would be justifiable to terminate the employment of an employee whose disability makes it impossible for him any longer to perform the main functions of his job, if an adjustment such as a move to a vacant post elsewhere in the business is not practicable or otherwise not reasonable for the employer to have to make.

It would be justifiable to terminate the employment of an employee with a worsening progressive condition if the increasing degree of adjustment necessary to accommodate the effects of the condition (shorter hours of work or falling productivity, say) became unreasonable for the employer to have to make.

An employer who needs to reduce the workforce would have to ensure that any scheme which was introduced for choosing candidates for redundancy did not discriminate against disabled people. Therefore, if a criterion for redundancy would apply to a disabled person for a reason relating to the disability, that criterion would have to be "material" and "substantial" and the employer would have to consider whether a reasonable adjustment would prevent the criterion applying to the disabled person after all.

Harassment

What does the Act say about harassment?

6.22 The Act does not refer to harassment as a separate issue. However, harassing a disabled person on account of a disability will almost always amount to a "detriment" under the Act. (Victimisation is covered in paragraphs 4.53–4.54).

Are employers liable for harassment by their employees?

6.23 An employer is responsible for acts of harassment by employees in the course of their employment unless the employer took such steps as were reasonable practicable to prevent it. As a minimum first step harassment because of disability should be made a disciplinary matter and staff should be made aware that it will be taken seriously.

Discrimination against contract workers

7.1   The Act deals specifically with work which is carried out by individuals ("contract workers") for a person (a "principal") who hires them under contract from their employer (generally an employment business) – referred to below as the "sending" employer.

What does the Act say about contract workers?

7.2   *The Act says* that it is unlawful for a principal to discriminate against a disabled person:

- in the terms on which the person is allowed to do the contract work;

- by not allowing the person to do, or continue to do, the contract work;

- in the way he affords the person access to, or by failing to afford him access to, benefits in relation to contract work; or

- by subjecting the person to any other detriment in relation to contract work *(S12(1))*.

7.3   *The Act and Regulations apply*, generally speaking, as if the principal were, or would be, the actual employer of the contract worker. Therefore, the same definition of "discrimination" – including the need to justify less favourable treatment – applies as for employers *(S12(3))*.

> The employer of a labourer, who some years ago was disabled by clinical depression but has since recovered, proposes to supply him to a contractor to work on a building site. Although his past disability is covered by the Act, the site manager refuses to accept him because of his medical history. Unless the contractor can show that the manager's action is justified, the contractor would be acting unlawfully.

What will be the effect of the duty to make adjustments for principals?

7.4   The duty to make a reasonable adjustment applies to a principal as to an employer *(S12(3))*.

7.5   In deciding whether any, and if so, what, adjustment would be reasonable for a principal to have to make, the period for which the contract worker will work for the principal is important. It might well be unreasonable for a principal to have to make certain adjustments if the worker will be with the principal for only a short time.

An employment business enters into a contract with a firm of accountants to provide an assistant for two weeks to cover an unexpected absence. The employment business wishes to put forward a person who, because of his disability, finds it difficult to travel during the rush hour and would like his working hours to be modified accordingly. It might not be reasonable for the firm to have to agree given the short time in which to negotiate and implement the new hours.

Will the principal and the "sending" employer both have duties to make reasonable adjustments?

7.6 Both the "sending" employer and the principal may separately be under a duty of reasonable adjustment in the case of a contract worker who is disabled. If the "sending" employer's own premises or arrangements place the contract worker at a substantial disadvantage, then the "sending" employer may have a duty to make a reasonable adjustment *(S6(1))*. The "sending" employer may also have a duty to make a reasonable adjustment where a similar substantial disadvantage is likely to affect a contract worker as a result of the arrangements or premises of all or most of the principals to whom he might be supplied. The employer would not have to take separate steps in relation to each principal, but would have to make any reasonable adjustment within his power which would overcome the disadvantage wherever it might arise. The principal would not have to make any adjustment which the employer should make.[15] However, subject to that the principal would be responsible only for any additional reasonable adjustment which is necessary solely because of the principal's own arrangements or premises *(S6(1)* applied by *S12(3))*. It would also usually be reasonable for a principal and a "sending" employer to have to cooperate with any steps taken by the other to assist a disabled contract worker.

A travel agency hires a clerical worker from an employment business to fulfil a three month contract to file travel invoices during the busy summer holiday period. The contract worker is a wheelchair user, and is quite capable of doing the job if a few minor, temporary changes are made to the arrangement of furniture in the office. It would be reasonable for the travel agency to make this adjustment.

15 Employment Regulations (see paragraph 1.6)

A bank hires a blind word processor operator as a contract worker from an employment business. The employment business provides her with a specially adapted portable computer because she would otherwise be at a similar substantial disadvantage in doing the work wherever she does it. (In such circumstances the bank would not have to provide a specially adapted computer if the employment business did not.) The bank would have to cooperate by letting the contract worker use her computer whilst working for the bank if it is compatible with the bank's systems. If not, it could be a reasonable adjustment for the bank to make the computer compatible and for the employment business to allow that change to be made.

What about contract workers in small firms?

7.7   The Act applies to any employment business which has 20 or more employees (including people currently employed by it but hired out to principals). It also applies to any principal who has 20 or more workers (counting both the principal's own employees and any contract workers currently working for the principal). It does not apply to employment businesses or principals with fewer than 20 employees. Note the extended definition of "employment" in the Act (see paragraph 2.8).

An employment business has 15 employees (including people currently hired out to others) and enters a contract to provide a worker in a shop. The shop employs 29 people. Neither the duty not to discriminate nor the duty to make a reasonable adjustment applies to the employment business, but both duties apply to the owner of the shop. However, the length of time the worker was contracted to work at the shop would be an important factor in assessing whether the shop-owner had to make any significant adjustment.

A deaf individual is employed by an employment business that has 100 employees (including people currently hired out to others). He is hired regularly to do contract work and, as a reasonable adjustment, the business provides a portable induction loop for assignments. If he works for a principal with, say, 17 workers, (counting both employees and contract workers) that principal would not be required to cooperate with use of the induction loop. However, if the principal has 20 or more such workers the principal would be obliged to cooperate.

What about the Supported Placement Scheme (SPS)?

7.8 These arrangements also apply to the Employment Service's Supported Placement Scheme (SPS) for severely disabled people. The "contractor" under the scheme (usually a local authority or voluntary body) is the equivalent of the "sending" employer, and the "host employer" is the equivalent of the principal. A local authority can even be both the contractor and the host employer at the same time (as can a voluntary body) in which case the duty not to discriminate and the duty of reasonable adjustment would apply to it as to an employer.

Provisions applying to trade organisations

What does the Act say about trade organisations?

7.9 A trade organisation is defined as an organisation of workers or of employers, or any other organisation whose members carry on a particular profession or trade for the purposes of which the organisation exists *(S13(4))*. Therefore trade unions, employers' associations, and similar bodies like the Law Society and chartered professional institutions, for example, must comply with the legislation.

7.10 *The Act says* that it is unlawful for a trade organisation to discriminate against a disabled person:

- in the terms on which it is prepared to admit the person to membership; or

- by refusing to accept, or deliberately not accepting, an application for membership.

It is also unlawful for a trade organisation to discriminate against a disabled member of the organisation:

- in the way it affords the person access to any benefits or by refusing or deliberately omitting to afford access to them;

- by depriving the person of membership, or varying the terms of membership; or

- by subjecting the person to any other detriment *(S13)*.

Trade organisations should therefore check that they do not discriminate as regards, for example, training facilities, welfare or insurance schemes, invitations to attend events, processing of grievances, assistance to members in their employers' disciplinary or dismissal procedures.

7.11 *The Act defines* discrimination by a trade organisation in similar terms to the definition relating to discrimination by an employer. Therefore, the need to justify less favourable treatment for a reason relating to disability applies as in the case of an employer *(S14(3))*.

> A trade organisation is arranging a trip to some of its members' workplaces but it decides to exclude a member in a wheelchair because too many of the sites are inaccessible to make participation worthwhile. This could well be justified. (Note, however, paragraph 7.12)

Do trade organisations have a duty to make adjustments?

7.12 *The Act includes* a requirement on trade organisations to make reasonable adjustments *(S15)*. However, this duty will not be brought into force until after the other employment provisions, at a date which will be subject to consultation.

What about the actions of employees or representatives of trade organisations?

7.13 Individual employees or agents of trade organisations who have dealings with members or applicants are treated in the same way as individual employees or agents of employers who deal with job applicants or employees: the trade organisation is responsible for their actions *(S58)*.

8 Resolving disagreements within the employing organisation

What does the Act say about resolving disagreements?

8.1   The Act does not require employers to resolve disputes within their organisations. However, it is in an employer's interests to resolve problems as they arise where possible. This should be in a non-discriminatory way to comply with the Act's general provisions.

8.2   One method might be the use of a grievance procedure. Grievance procedures provide an open and fair way for employees to make known their concerns and enable grievances to be resolved quickly before they become major difficulties. Use of the procedures can highlight areas where the employer's duty of reasonable adjustment may not have been observed, and can prevent misunderstandings in this area leading to tribunal complaints.

Do existing grievance and disciplinary procedures need changing?

8.3   Where grievance or disciplinary procedures are in place, the employer might wish to review, and where necessary adapt, them to ensure that they are flexible enough to be used by disabled employees. Where a formal grievance (or disciplinary) procedure operates, it must be open, or applied, to disabled employees on the same basis as to others. Employers will have to ensure that grievance (or disciplinary) procedures do not, in themselves, discriminate against disabled employees and may have to make reasonable adjustments to enable some disabled employees to use grievance procedures effectively or to ensure disciplinary procedures have the same impact on disabled employees as on others.

> An employee with a learning disability has to attend an interview under the employer's disciplinary procedures. The employee would like his guardian or a friend to be present. The employer agrees to this but refuses to rearrange the interview to a time which is more convenient to the guardian or friend. The employer may be in breach of the duty to make a reasonable adjustment.

(See Annex 3 for information about industrial tribunals.)

1   **This Annex is included to aid understanding about who is covered by the Act and should provide sufficient information on the definition of disability to cover the large majority of cases. The definition of disability in the Act is designed to cover only people who would generally be considered to be disabled. A Government publication *Guidance on matters to be taken into account in determining questions relating to the definition of disability*, is also available.**

When is a person disabled?

2   A person has a disability if he has a physical or mental impairment which has a substantial and long-term adverse effect on his ability to carry out normal day-to-day activities.

What about people who have recovered from a disability?

3   People who have had a disability within the definition are protected from discrimination even if they have since recovered.

What does "impairment" cover?

4   It covers physical or mental impairments; this includes sensory impairments, such as those affecting sight or hearing.

Are all mental impairments covered?

5   The term "mental impairment" is intended to cover a wide range of impairments relating to mental functioning, including what are often known as learning disabilities. However, the Act states that it does not include any impairment resulting from or consisting of a mental illness, unless that illness is a clinically well-recognised illness. A clinically well-recognised illness is one that is recognised by a respected body of medical opinion.

What is a "substantial" adverse effect?

6   A substantial adverse effect is something which is more than a minor or trivial effect. The requirement that an effect must be substantial reflects the general understanding of disability as a limitation going beyond the normal differences in ability which might exist among people.

What is a "long-term" effect?

7   A long-term effect of an impairment is one:

- which has lasted at least 12 months; or

- where the total period for which it lasts is likely to be at least 12 months; or

- which is likely to last for the rest of the life of the person affected.

8   Effects which are not long-term would therefore include loss of mobility due to a broken limb which is likely to heal within 12 months and the effects of temporary infections, from which a person would be likely to recover within 12 months.

What if the effects come and go over a period of time?

9   If an impairment has had a substantial adverse effect on normal day-to-day activities but that effect ceases, the substantial effect is treated as continuing if it is likely to recur; that is if it is more probable than not that the effect will *recur*. To take the example of a person with rheumatoid arthritis whose impairment has a substantial adverse effect, which then ceases to be substantial (i.e. the person has a period of remission). The effects are to be treated as if they are continuing, and are likely to continue beyond 12 months, *if:*

- the impairment remains; and

- at least one recurrence of the substantial effect is likely to take place 12 months or more after the initial occurrence.

This would then be a long-term effect.

What are "normal day-to-day activities"?

10   They are activities which are carried out by most people on a fairly regular and frequent basis. The term is not intended to include activities which are normal only for a particular person or group of people, such as playing a musical instrument, or a sport, to a professional standard or performing a skilled or specialised task at work. However, someone who is affected in such a specialised way but is *also* affected in normal day-to-day activities, would be covered by this part of the definition. The test of whether an impairment affects normal day-to-day activities is whether it affects one of the broad categories of capacity listed in Schedule 1 to the Act. They are:

- mobility;

- manual dexterity;

- physical co-ordination;

- continence;

- ability to lift, carry or otherwise move everyday objects;

- speech, hearing or eyesight;

- memory or ability to concentrate, learn or understand; or

- perception of the risk of physical danger.

What about treatment?

11   Someone with an impairment may be receiving medical or other treatment which alleviates or removes the effects (though not the impairment). In such cases, the treatment is ignored and the impairment is taken to have the effect it would have had without such treatment. This does not apply if substantial adverse effects are not likely to recur even if the treatment stops (i.e. the impairment has been cured).

Does this include people who wear spectacles?

12   No. The sole exception to the rule about ignoring the effects of treatment is the wearing of spectacles or contact lenses. In this case, the effect while the person is wearing spectacles or contact lenses should be considered.

Are people who have disfigurements covered?

13   People with severe disfigurements are covered by the Act. They do not need to demonstrate that the impairment has a substantial adverse effect on their ability to carry out normal day-to-day activities.

What about people who know their condition is going to get worse over time?

14   Progressive conditions are conditions which are likely to change and develop over time. Examples given in the Act are cancer, multiple sclerosis, muscular dystrophy and HIV infection. Where a person has a progressive condition he will be covered by the Act from the moment the condition leads to an impairment which has *some* effect on ability to carry out normal day-to-day activities, even though not a *substantial* effect, if that impairment is likely eventually to have a substantial adverse effect on such ability.

What about people who are registered disabled?

15   Those registered as disabled under the Disabled Persons (Employment) Act 1944 both on 12 January 1995 and 2 December 1996 will be treated as being disabled under the Disability Discrimination Act 1995 for three years from the latter date. At all times from 2 December 1996 onwards they will be covered by the Act as people who have had a disability. This does not preclude them from being covered as having a current disability any time after the three year period has finished. Whether they are or not will depend on whether they – like anyone else – meet the definition of disability in the Act.

Are people with genetic conditions covered?

16   If a genetic condition has no effect on ability to carry out normal day-to-day activities, the person is not covered. Diagnosis does not in itself bring someone within the definition. If the condition is progressive, then the rule about progressive conditions applies.

Are any conditions specifically excluded from the coverage of the Act?

17   Yes. Certain conditions are to be regarded as not amounting to impairments for the purposes of the Act. These are:

- addiction to or dependency on alcohol, nicotine, or any other substance (other than as a result of the substance being medically prescribed);

- seasonal allergic rhinitis (e.g. hayfever), except where it aggravates the effect of another condition;

- tendency to set fires;

- tendency to steal;

- tendency to physical or sexual abuse of other persons;

- exhibitionism;

- voyeurism.

Also, disfigurements which consist of a tattoo (which has not been removed), non-medical body piercing, or something attached through such piercing, are to be treated as not having a substantial adverse effect on the person's ability to carry out normal day-to-day activities.[16]

16 Definition Regulations (see paragraph 1.6)

1   A range of leaflets about various aspects of the Act is available. To obtain copies, call 0345 622 633 (local rate), or textphone 0345 622 644. Copies of the leaflets are also available in braille and audio cassette.

2   Statutory Guidance on the definition of disability is produced separately. This can be obtained from HMSO bookshops – see back cover of this Code. This Guidance should prove helpful where it is not clear whether or not a person has or has had a disability.

3   There is a wide range of practical help and advice available to assist employers in the recruitment and employment of people, including disabled people, for example from Jobcentres, Careers Service offices, Training and Enterprise Councils (in England and Wales) and Local Enterprise Companies (in Scotland). Addresses and telephone numbers are available in local telephone directories.

4   Where necessary, specialist help and advice for disabled people and for employers who might, or do, employ disabled people is available from the Employment Service through its local Placing, Assessment and Counselling Teams (PACTs). PACTs can help with issues related to employing disabled people, but cannot advise on an employer's specific legal obligations.

5   PACTs may be able to provide help with special aids, equipment and other measures to overcome the effects of disability in the working environment.

6   The addresses and telephone numbers of PACTs are listed in local telephone directories under "Employment Service", or can be obtained from the nearest Jobcentre.

7   Many specialist organisations for disabled people also offer a range of employment help and advice. The Employment Service publish a booklet called Sources of Information and Advice (Ref: PGP6) which lists many of the specialist organisations offering help to employers on employment and disability issues. The booklet can be obtained from PACTs.

8   The Advisory, Conciliation and Arbitration Service (ACAS) can help employers and individuals with factual information on the legislation and assistance related to its effects on industrial relations practices and procedures. The address and telephone numbers of ACAS offices are listed in local telephone directories under "ACAS".

9   Employers working in historic buildings, or other heritage properties, may also wish to obtain a copy of *Easy Access to Historic Properties* from English Heritage at 23 Savile Row, London W1X 1AB.
Tel: 0171 973 3434.

10   Disability can take a very large number of forms and the action an employer may be required to take will depend to a very large extent on the particular circumstances of the case. Any advice and information employers receive should be considered in that light. In some circumstances employers may wish to consider whether they should seek legal advice.

What does the Act say about making complaints?

1   **The Act says** that a person who believes that an employer has unlawfully discriminated or failed to make a reasonable adjustment, or that a person has aided an employer to do such an act, may present a complaint to an industrial tribunal **(S8(1))**.

What does the Act say about conciliation?

2   When a formal complaint has been made to an industrial tribunal **the Act places a duty** on the Advisory, Conciliation and Arbitration Service's (ACAS) conciliation officers to try to promote settlement of the dispute without a tribunal hearing **(Sch 3, Para 1)**. ACAS can also assist in this way without a formal application to a tribunal being made.

What does the Act say about obtaining a remedy for unlawful discrimination?

3   **The Act says** that a disabled person who believes someone has unlawfully discriminated against him or failed to make a reasonable adjustment, in breach of the employment provisions of the Act or Regulations, may present a complaint to an industrial tribunal **(S8(1))**.

4   If the tribunal upholds the complaint it may:

   ■ declare the rights of the disabled person (the complainant), and the other person (the respondent) in relation to the complaint;

   ■ order the other person to pay the complainant compensation; and

   ■ recommend that, within a specified time, the other person take reasonable action to prevent or reduce the adverse effect in question **(S8(2))**.

5   **The Act allows** compensation for injury to feelings to be awarded whether or not other compensation is awarded **(S8(4))**.

6   **The Act says** that if a respondent fails, without reasonable justification, to comply with an industrial tribunal's recommendation, the tribunal may:

   ■ increase the amount of compensation to be paid; or

   ■ order the respondent to pay compensation if it did not make such an order earlier **(S8(5))**.

Who can be taken to an Industrial Tribunal?

7   The tribunal complaints procedure applies to anyone who, it is claimed, has discriminated in the employment field – employers (and their employees and agents for whose acts they are responsible), trade organisations, people who hire contract workers and people who aid any of these to discriminate.

Complaints involving landlords

8   If a reasonable adjustment requiring the consent of the employer's landlord (or a superior landlord) is not made, for whatever reason, the disabled person may bring a complaint against the employer in an industrial tribunal. Either the disabled person or the employer may ask the tribunal to make the landlord a party to the proceedings. If the industrial tribunal finds that the landlord acted unreasonably in withholding consent, or gave consent but attached an unreasonable condition, it can make any appropriate declaration, order that the alteration may be made, or award compensation against the landlord ***(S27 and Sch 4 Para 2)***.

Complaining about pension schemes

9   A disabled person who considers that the trustees or managers of a pension scheme have discriminated against him, may complain through the pensions dispute resolution mechanism. Information about the scheme should give details about this. If necessary, a complaint may be made to the Pensions Ombudsman.

10   From April 1997, all occupational pension schemes will be required to set up and operate procedures for resolving disputes between individual pension scheme members and the trustees or managers.

11   The Occupational Pensions Advisory Service (OPAS) can provide an advice and conciliation service for members of the public who have problems with their occupational pension. OPAS can be contacted at 11 Belgrave Road, London SW1U 1RB. Tel: 0171 233 8080.

12   A disabled person who considers that an employer has discriminated against him in providing access to a pension scheme can complain to an industrial tribunal following the same process for other complaints against employers.

What is the "Questionnaire Procedure"?

13. *The Act provides for* a procedure (the questionnaire procedure) to assist a person who believes that discrimination has occurred, to decide whether or not to start proceedings and, if the person does, to formulate and present a case in the most effective manner *(S56)*. Questionnaire forms will be obtainable from Jobcentres.

Can compromise agreements be an alternative to making tribunal complaints?

14 *The Act says* that, in general, the terms of an agreement (such as a contract of employment) cannot prevent a disabled person from complaining to an industrial tribunal, or force a complaint to be stopped *(S9)*. However, *the Act also says* that in some circumstances a disabled person can make an agreement not to make a complaint or to stop one *(S9)*.

15 These circumstances are if:

■ an ACAS conciliation officer has acted under the Act on the matter; *or* the following conditions apply:

■ the disabled person must have received independent legal advice from a qualified lawyer about the terms and effects of the agreement, particularly its effect on his ability to complain to a tribunal;

■ the adviser must have an insurance policy covering any loss arising from the advice; and

■ the agreement must be in writing, relate to the complaint, identify the adviser and say that these conditions are satisfied.

16 It may be in the interests of some disabled people to make such "compromise" agreements instead of pursuing complaints to industrial tribunal hearings, but care should be taken to ensure that the above conditions are met.

How is a complaint made to an Industrial Tribunal?

17   Complaints to an industrial tribunal can be made on an application form (IT1). Forms are obtainable from Jobcentres. Completed applications should be returned to the Industrial Tribunals Central Office. The address is on the form.

18   Applications to an industrial tribunal must be made within three months of the time when the incident being complained of occurred. The time limit will not normally be extended to allow for the time it might take to try to settle the dispute within the organisation eg. by way of internal grievance procedures (see paragraphs 8.1–8.3). A tribunal may, however, consider a complaint which is out of time, if it considers, in all the circumstances of the case, that it is just and equitable to do so *(Sch 3, Para 3)*.

What does the Act say about reporting restrictions?

19   *The Act empowers* a tribunal to make "restricted reporting orders" if it considers that evidence of a personal nature is likely to be heard by the tribunal. Such orders prohibit the publication, for example in a newspaper, of any matter likely to lead members of the public to identify the complainant or any other person mentioned in the order, until the tribunal's decision is promulgated.

Index

References are to paragraph numbers (including the associated examples) in this Code and its annexes. References to specific disabilities in the examples contained in the Code are not shown separately in the index. The examples are illustrative only (see paragraph 3.1) and it could be misleading to suggest that particular examples apply only to the type of disability specifically mentioned in them. The approach taken in this index is to refer to the kinds of situations which employers might face in relation to the employment of disabled people or to particular provisions in the Act. Cross references to other index items are given in brackets. References to "the Act" are to the Disability Discrimination Act 1995.